SIERRA CLUB
WILDLIFE
LIBRARY

APES

SIERRA CLUB
WILDLIFE
LIBRARY

APES

Eric S. Grace

General Editor, R. D. Lawrence

Sierra Club Books for Children
San Francisco

First Edition

Photo credits: © Nancy Adams / Tom Stack & Associates, 34; © K. & K. Ammann, 13; © K. & K. Ammann / Planet Earth Pictures, 23, 30, 59; © Yann Arthus-Bertrand / Auscape International, 21; © Erwin & Peggy Bauer, 46; © Rod Brindamour / Orangutan Foundation International, 9; © Robert M. Campbell / National Geographic Image Collection, 8; © John Cancalosi, 7; © John Cancalosi / Auscape International, 15; © John Cancalosi / Tom Stack & Associates, 5; © Alain Compost / Bios, 50; © Ferrero/Labat / Auscape International, 11, 24; © John Guistina / The Wildlife Collection, 16, 35; © Michel Gunther / Bios, 26, 31; © Martin Harvey / The Wildlife Collection, 28, 32; © George Holton / Photo Researchers, 3; © Brian Kenney / Planet Earth Pictures, 27; © Frans Lanting / First Light, 1, 62; © Wayne Lawler / Auscape International, 53; © Wayne Lynch, 37, 61; © Joe McDonald, 41; © Brian Parker / Tom Stack & Associates, 47, 54; © Inga Spence / Tom Stack & Associates, 57; © Roy Toft / Tom Stack & Associates, 44; © Steve Turner / Auscape International, 39; © Kennan Ward / Bruce Coleman Inc., 10

Library of Congress Cataloging-in-Publication Data

Grace, Eric S.
 Apes / Eric S. Grace ; general editor, R.D. Lawrence. – 1st ed.
  p.   cm. – (Sierra Club wildlife library)
 Includes index.
 ISBN 0-87156-365-7
 1. Apes – Juvenile literature. [1. Apes.]   I. Lawrence, R.D.,
1921-   .   II. Title.   III. Series.
QL737.P96G65   1995
599.88 — dc20   95-2167

Published in Canada by Key Porter Books Limited, Toronto, Ontario

Printed in Canada

10 9 8 7 6 5 4 3 2 1

Contents

Into the Forests

Whenever I watch apes at the zoo, there always seem to be visitors who can't resist aping the apes. They jump up and down and hoot and scratch themselves, looking like chimpanzees who have escaped from their enclosures and put on clothes.

Watching apes and people together, it's easy to see haunting similarities. But these similarities are not surprising to zoologists. We look like chimpanzees, gorillas, and orangutans because we *are* like them. Our blood is so similar that we could safely get a transfusion from a chimpanzee. Our bones and genes are alike. We suffer from the same diseases. It takes an expert to see any differences between the skeleton of a baby ape and that of a human baby. Even the brain cases of humans and gorillas are the same size at birth.

We are so close, in fact, that zoologists now group chimpanzees, gorillas, and orangutans in the same family with humans – the family *Hominidae* (hom-IN-ee-dee), also known as the *great apes*. (Gibbons are sometimes called *lesser apes*.)

If you wanted to see a great ape in the wild, you'd have to journey to tropical Africa or Southeast Asia. You would then take a long and difficult trek into the forests where they make their homes. Until the 1800s, very few Europeans or North Americans had ever seen an ape. All that most people knew about them came from the reports of traders and explorers, who made up stories from brief glimpses of wild apes or from encounters they had while hunting. Many travelers wrote scary tales describing apes as giant, hairy animals with human faces. Some even claimed apes could speak and build huts.

Another view of apes arose when Charles Darwin's book, *The Origin of Species*, was published in 1859. The book described Darwin's theory of natural

The skeleton of a baby gorilla is very similar to that of a human baby.

Dian Fossey began studying mountain gorillas in Rwanda in 1966.

selection and explained how living things change over time through the process of evolution. It implied that human beings must also have evolved – from apelike ancestors. Many people were shocked by this idea. Many misunderstood Darwin. They thought he was saying that people evolved from chimpanzees or gorillas. But the great apes living today also evolved from earlier ancestors. They are not our great-grandparents, but our cousins.

It took nearly a hundred years after Darwin wrote his book until scientists set out to observe apes in the wild. Oddly enough, it was an anthropologist – a scientist who studies humans – who began to get people interested in wild apes. Dr. Louis Leakey had discovered many fossil remains of extinct, human-like creatures in East Africa. These fossil bones tell us what our ancestors looked like millions of years ago.

Biruté Galdikas began her work with orangutans in Borneo in 1969.

But to really understand who we are, Leakey thought, we must learn about the behavior of our closest living relatives. During the 1960s, he encouraged three remarkable women to go into the forests, watch apes, and take notes.

Much of what we know today about wild apes is based on the pioneering work of these women, who spent many years making patient observations. Jane Goodall began studying chimpanzees in Tanzania, East Africa, in 1960. Dian Fossey started her work on mountain gorillas in Rwanda in 1966. And Biruté Galdikas went to Borneo to study orangutans in 1969. After centuries of myths and misunderstandings, people were at last learning some fascinating facts about the lives of the great apes.

In addition to studies of apes in the forest, scientists found startling evidence that we are closer

9

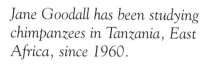

Jane Goodall has been studying chimpanzees in Tanzania, East Africa, since 1960.

to apes than anyone had imagined. By comparing human and ape genes, scientists found that chimpanzees and people differ by less than 2 percent. In fact, chimpanzees are more closely related to humans than they are to gorillas.

What makes humans unique? Not the ability to use tools, because chimpanzees regularly make and use tools. Not language, because all apes have the ability to learn language. Not even culture, because groups of apes also pass on their traditional ways of doing things from generation to generation. What sets us apart is not any of these things alone, but rather the huge scale on which we use our tools, language, and culture.

For most of human history, we differed very little from chimpanzees, gorillas, and orangutans. Our numbers were few and our tools were simple and made of stone or bone. We have shared millions of years on this planet with the apes. By returning to the forests to learn about them, we are also discovering more about ourselves.

Wild chimpanzees use tools to get food. This one is fishing termites from their nest with a piece of dry grass.

Primate Beginnings

Scientists include humans and great apes – together with gibbons, monkeys, marmosets, bush babies, tarsiers, lorises, and lemurs – in a group of animals called *primates* (see pages 18–19). Most primates live in tropical and subtropical forests in Central and South America, Africa, and Asia. They range in size from the pygmy marmoset of the Amazon jungle, which weighs less than 3 ounces, to the gorilla, which tips the scales at more than 400 pounds.

Despite the variety in their appearance, however, all primates have several things in common, including big, complicated brains, and hands that can grip and hold things. To understand why large brains and grasping hands are important, you must travel back to a time when there were no monkeys or apes on Earth.

About 65 million years ago, the Age of Reptiles was coming to an end. The giant dinosaurs were extinct, and birds and mammals were taking the place of reptiles in forests, swamps, and deserts around the world. On forest floors, many different types of ratlike mammals competed for food and shelter. Some of them hid or hunted in burrows or under fallen logs. Others began climbing into bushes or small trees, where they not only escaped their enemies but also found plenty of insects, leaves, and fruits to eat. The ability to climb helped them survive. Among the animals that adapted to life in the trees were the ancestors of today's monkeys and apes.

Imagine the challenges faced by one of these animals as it searched for a meal along branches high above the ground. Food or enemies could be anywhere in the treetop world – above or below, as well as in front or behind. To meet this challenge, early primates developed large, forward-facing eyes with color and stereoscopic (three-dimensional) vision. Seeing colors

*Hand-eye coordination requires
a large, complex brain.*

HOW PRIMATES SEE IN STEREO

Primates can see in three dimensions because each eye has a slightly different view of the same scene. You can see this for yourself by trying an experiment. Stand a large picture book upright on a table and place an object, such as an apple, in front of it. Sit quite still and look at the apple with one eye, then the other eye, and rapidly switch back and forth between eyes a few times. The apple will seem to jump from side to side in front of the book. When you use both eyes, your brain merges the two overlapping images into a single stereo-scopic (or three-dimensional) view that shows how far away the apple is from the book and from you.

helped them find ripe fruit or brightly patterned insects among the ocean of green leaves. Stereoscopic vision made them good judges of distance, so they could jump from branch to branch with little risk of missing their aim and falling.

While sight was vital for the early primates' survival, the sense of smell was less important in the trees than on the ground. The noses of early primates became smaller and less sensitive than the long snouts of ground-sniffers such as dogs and rats. The combination of a short nose and forward-facing eyes is what gives most monkeys and apes their flat, human-like faces.

Along with adaptations in the primates' senses came changes in the ways they moved around.

The ease with which they climbed, swung, ran, and jumped through the treetops were all thanks to the development of their remarkable hands and feet. Compare your own hands, which are typical of a primate's, with the paws of a dog or cat. Our palms do not have thick pads for walking on the ground, but thin skin that is sensitive to touch. We do not have claws, but flat nails that leave our fingertips exposed for touching. Our fingers are not joined together by webs of skin, but are long and separate. Our thumbs can be moved around to face our fingers, letting us grip objects between our thumb and fingers or wrap our hands firmly around things.

It would be hard to exaggerate the importance of hands to the success of monkeys and apes. Flexible, gripping hands give primates the ability to handle their world with precision and power. Hands make it possible for primates to pick up objects as small as seeds or as big as rocks. Hands let them hold things, turn them, carry them, throw them, pull them apart, and put them together.

As the eyes and hands of early primates evolved, so did their brains. The parts of the brain controlling vision and touch got bigger, while the parts dealing with the sense of smell got smaller. Primates developed good coordination, a good memory, and flexible behavior. Their brains grew larger and more complex. Monkeys and apes became the intelligent and curious animals we see today.

Life in the trees brought other changes in the bodies of some primates. Their back legs became stronger, so they could leap from bough to bough. Their posture grew more upright as they stood on branches and plucked at fruits and leaves above them. Some primates swung from branch to branch hanging by their arms. This Tarzan-like way of moving led them to develop very long, strong arms and hooklike hands.

The forward-facing eyes and short nose of this gorilla give it the typical look of a primate face.

Most primates have only one
offspring at a time.

Another result of life in the trees is that primates have small families. Imagine trying to carry eight or nine babies while running along a branch! Most primates have just one baby at a time. They have only two nipples for suckling their offspring, unlike many other mammals, which have two rows of nipples. Another reason for primates' small families is that their young have a lot to learn. Parents must spend several years teaching each youngster where to find food, how to avoid danger, ways of cooperating with other members of their group, and so on.

The most recent chapter in the history of primates started about 26 million years ago, when Earth's climate grew hotter and drier. Large areas of forest died, and grasslands took their place. Just as the treetops had once presented a new opportunity for early primates millions of years before, now the grasslands offered possibilities to explore. Larger primates began living on the ground, confident of defending themselves away from the shelter of trees. By 20 million years ago, the ancestors of baboons, macaques, and great apes had taken shape on the African savannas.

Today, there are about 230 species of primates in the world. They can be grouped into two broad types. The *prosimians*, or "early monkeys," include lemurs, lorises, bush babies, and tarsiers. They live in Africa and Asia and are generally small and active at night. *Anthropoids* include apes and the larger monkeys, most of which are active only during the day.

THE PRIMATES

There are two main groups, or suborders, of primates: the prosimians and the anthropoids.

PROSIMIANS

Lemurs

There are five families of lemurs, all of which live on the island of Madagascar. They range from the five-inch-long mouse lemur to the three-foot-long indri – the largest of the prosimians. There are about thirty species of lemurs.

Ring-tailed lemur

Lorises

Lorises are slow-moving primates that live in the tropical forests of Southeast Asia. They sleep in trees during the day and hunt for insects and other small animals at night. Also included in this family are the potto and angwantibo of Africa. There are only six species in the family.

Slender loris

Bush babies

Bush babies, or galagos, are small, swift-moving animals that leap from branch to branch chasing insects in the African forests. They have huge, round eyes that help them see at night. There are eleven species of galagos.

Bush baby

Western tarsier

Tarsiers

Tarsiers have round heads, enormous eyes, and big ears that are constantly moving. These swift, small (less than six inches long) primates live in dense forests on several islands in Southeast Asia. There are six species of tarsiers.

Marmoset

ANTHROPOIDS

Marmosets and tamarins

These small animals, many with vivid colors and markings, scamper like squirrels through the Amazon forests of South America. They feed on insects, fruits, and berries. Tamarins differ from marmosets by having longer canine teeth, which look like small tusks, on their lower jaws. There are twenty-six species.

New World monkeys
The fifty-eight species that make up this family of primates live mainly in South America. They can be distinguished from Old World monkeys by their nostrils, which open forward and are set wide apart. The group includes capuchin monkeys, squirrel monkeys, woolly monkeys, spider monkeys, and Goeldi's monkey.

Black-handed gibbon

Gorilla

Gibbons
Gibbons, sometimes called lesser apes, are acrobatic primates with long, slender arms that enable them to swing from branch to branch. All eleven species live in Southeast Asia.

Woolly monkey

Old World monkeys
The eighty-one species of Old World monkeys live in Africa and Asia. They all have noses with nostrils turned downward. Some have tails; others do not. Many of them grow quite large and spend much of their time on the ground. Others live mainly in trees. They include colobus monkeys, macaques, mangabeys, baboons, langurs, and the proboscis and Patas monkeys.

Chimpanzee

Great apes
The two species of chimpanzee, together with the gorilla, orangutan, and human, make up the five species of great apes. They are the largest primates.

Yellow baboon

Orangutan

Almost Human: Chimpanzees

One thing you can say about chimpanzees, concludes Jane Goodall, is that they are as complicated and unpredictable in their behavior as people. Researchers in East Africa discovered just how surprising chimps can be during the 1970s, when a new and shocking behavior suddenly appeared among a community of chimpanzees they had been observing for ten years.

The community of about fifty animals lived along a river valley near Gombe, Tanzania. They had always appeared peaceful and cooperative with one another. But suddenly, some of the chimpanzees began to attack and kill other chimps. What had happened?

The attacks began after nine of the chimpanzees moved to a nearby valley to start a new group of their own. Soon after they left, males from the larger community set out on raids to hunt the breakaway chimps. Groups of five or six males would wait until they found a chimp alone, then brutally attack it. After a raid, the hunters returned to their area of the forest, leaving their badly injured victim to die. The raids and attacks continued for about six years, stopping only when the smaller community had completely disappeared.

Some people have compared this puzzling and unusual behavior to warfare. Hunting and killing, together with tool use, are two of the things that chimpanzees and humans have in common — and two things that make them different from the other great apes. Whatever the explanation for the chimpanzees' aggressive actions, there's no doubt that if the research had stopped before 1970, our picture of chimpanzees today would be quite different.

Chimpanzees are the smallest of the great apes. Adult males stand just under five feet tall and weigh about 100 pounds, whereas females are a little shorter

Chimpanzees are as complicated and unpredictable in their behavior as people.

THE TWO SPECIES OF CHIMPANZEE

There are two species of chimpanzee: the common chimpanzee and the bonobo, or pygmy chimpanzee. Common chimpanzees live in western and central Africa, north of the Zaire River. Bonobos are found only in the rain forests of Central Zaire, south of the Zaire River. They are smaller than common chimpanzees, with blacker faces and smaller ears. The hair on a bonobo's head looks as if it has been parted along the center and combed down on either side. The bonobo's behavior and way of life are also slightly different from the common chimpanzee's. Most of the information in this chapter describes common chimpanzees.

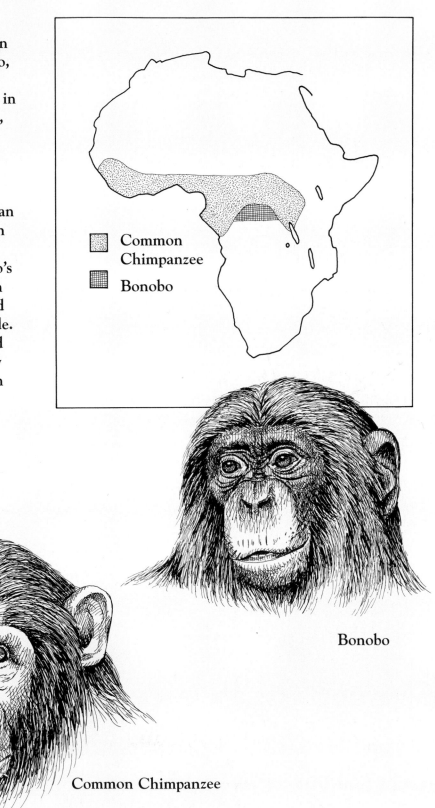

Common Chimpanzee
Bonobo
Bonobo

and lighter. They are very strong for their size. A chimp can pull a load of more than 800 pounds with only one hand.

Unlike most primates, chimpanzees don't live in tightly knit units. They form large, loose communities of thirty to seventy individuals, which break down into smaller groups. A group may be made up only of males or of females with their young, or it may be a mixed group of males and females of all ages. Each group changes frequently as some chimps leave and new ones join.

The chimpanzees in a community share the same broad area of forest, called their *home range*. The boundaries of this range are not rigid and may overlap with the ranges of neighboring communities. The size of a home range varies according to the type of forest where the chimpanzees live. In thick tropical forests, where trees grow close together and food is plentiful, the home range may be as small as two square miles. In open woodlands with scattered trees, chimpanzees need more room to find their food. During the course of a year, they may wander over a range of a hundred square miles or more.

Chimpanzees spend about six hours a day feeding and another two hours traveling from one feeding site to the next. They may eat at any time of the day (or even at night if there is bright moonlight), but they do most of their feeding shortly after sunrise and just before sunset. They eat a wide variety of things, including fruits and other parts of plants, insects, birds' eggs, honey, and small animals such as chicks, monkeys, and young bushbuck.

Chimps may look for fruits and insects on their own, but they cooperate in small groups to hunt animal prey. In Tanzania, their favorite prey is monkeys, which they may start stalking from as far away as a third of a mile. Their strategy is to chase

Chimpanzees live in constantly changing groups.

Chimpanzees are opportunistic feeders – they eat almost any food that is available.

the monkeys into an isolated clump of trees from which they cannot escape. The hunt can be long and deliberate, lasting up to two hours.

After a kill, the hunters gather around their prey, quarreling and hooting as they pull it apart. Those who eat the most meat are not necessarily those who made the kill. Large males get first choice, but they sometimes share the prey with smaller members of the group. Chimpanzees chew meat slowly, often with wads of leaves in their mouths.

The feeding habits of chimpanzees help explain why they live in small, ever-changing groups. Imagine a whole community of fifty or more chimps looking for food together. If they arrived at a fruit tree all at once, they would soon strip the tree of food and perhaps damage it. Fifty chimpanzees could not all sit together patiently fishing termites from a few termite hills. A nest of birds' eggs or a young bush pig would not go far among so many. In other words, if the entire community tried to feed together, many of them would run the risk of starving. On the other hand, by regularly keeping in touch with others in

THE RIGHT TOOL FOR THE JOB

Chimpanzees regularly use tools to help them get food. For example, to fish termites from their tunnels deep inside a termite mound, a chimp holds one end of a grass stem and pokes the other end into the mound. The termites attack the stem and hold on to it with their jaws. The chimp then carefully pulls out the stem with the termites still attached and picks them off with its lips.

Not just any old stem will do for a tool. A grass stem used for termite fishing must be long enough to reach the insects, but not so long that it will bend too much. It cannot be too brittle or it will break. It cannot be too stiff or it will not slide around corners. It must be smooth to slip down the narrow tunnels without sticking. A chimpanzee may sort through many different stems before getting one it likes, and it may carry the tool several yards to where it is to be used. Chimps sometimes keep spare stems on the ground or tucked in their laps.

Grooming reinforces social bonds between chimpanzees – in addition to removing burrs and parasites from their fur.

their community, small groups and individuals can cooperate in hunts and share information about good sources of food. By frequently splitting up and regrouping, chimpanzees use the varied resources of their environment more efficiently.

The chimps in a community know each other well and keep in touch by calls that can be heard a mile or more away. Each chimp has its own personality and rank, and serious fights within a community are rare. Bonding between them is very important. When chimps meet after being separated for a time, they greet one another with hugs, pats, kisses, and hoots. Most members of the community are related, but, as in human societies, chimpanzees get along better with some than with others. Close companions spend more time together, hold hands, and groom one another to show their trust.

This chimpanzee is grimacing because it is uneasy about something.

Researchers can recognize more than thirty different sounds chimpanzees make to express themselves. They grunt or make soft hooing noises when contented. They hoot loudly to announce the discovery of food. They bark, pant-hoot, and scream when they are excited, angry, or frightened. Because their voice box and tongue are not as flexible as a human's, chimpanzees are physically unable to make the wider range of sounds that we use in speech.

Like people, chimpanzees also communicate through their faces and body language. Staring is a threat. An expression that looks like a grin, with lips drawn back from the teeth, means the chimp is anxious or excited. Angry chimps raise their body hair up stiffly. An aggressive chimp swaggers, waves his arms, or hunches his shoulders. A nervous or fearful chimp has flattened hair and may crouch or bob up and down in front of a more dominant one.

*The bond between a mother
chimpanzee and her offspring
lasts throughout their lives.*

Bonds between mothers and their offspring continue throughout life. Every chimpanzee knows its own mother and keeps a close relationship with her. Fathers, on the other hand, take no part in raising their young and probably can't tell their own offspring from another's.

When a female chimpanzee is ready to mate, she develops a pinkish-red swelling at her posterior end. While in this state, she may be eagerly followed by as many as a dozen males. She doesn't choose one particular male, but may mate with several of them over a period of a few weeks.

About eight months after mating, the female gives birth to a tiny baby. Sometimes twins or even triplets are born, but usually only one of them survives. The care a baby gets during the first few years of life can make a difference to its future. Capable mothers with a high rank in the community raise confident and successful offspring. Less able mothers often raise chimpanzees with poor social skills.

For the first four years of life, a baby chimp stays close to its mother. It suckles her milk, rides on her back, and sleeps with her at night. Chimpanzees sleep in trees on nests made from leafy branches. They build new nests every night, each taking about five minutes to weave a springy platform in the fork of a tree. Before settling down for the night, they snap off uncomfortable twigs and may pile bunches of leaves under their heads to make pillows. All chimps (except babies) make their own nests.

As a baby chimp gets older and ventures farther from its mother's side, other members of the community share in its training. While their mothers feed, youngsters often play together, chasing one another, wrestling, tumbling, screaming, and generally acting much like human toddlers. Up to half the

Young chimps often gather in groups and play together as adults feed nearby.

chimpanzees in a community may be subadults, ranging in age from newborn infants to adolescents.

A mother won't have a second baby until her first is at least four or five years old. Up to the age of about seven, young chimps stay within sight or sound of their mothers but slowly grow more independent. Young males start to spend time with adult males. They become more aggressive and try to dominate others. Young females continue to live close to their mothers, learning how to look after infants. By the age of eight or nine, a chimpanzee is ready to take its place in the larger community away from its mother.

As teenagers, male chimpanzees join groups of adult males and show an interest in mating with females. By the time they are fifteen, they can dominate even adult females, but they continue to develop their place in the male hierarchy for several more years. Young teenage females may join groups of males and mate with them but are not mature enough

to become pregnant until they are about fourteen. Adolescent females often travel to neighboring communities when they are ready to mate. They may stay in a new community or travel back and forth between the two.

Females spend the years from their mid-teens to their early thirties raising young. A female may have as many as four, or rarely five, offspring during her life.

In his early twenties, a young adult chimpanzee is in his prime. He patrols his home range, often venturing to its borders. He tries to raise his status among other males during squabbles over food or females. By the age of thirty, his glossy black coat begins to turn brown on his back and legs, but he is still vigorous.

As a chimpanzee grows older, it becomes less active and gradually withdraws from social life. Its coat fades and may turn gray, its hair thins, and its teeth become worn and broken. Many older animals

A female chimpanzee may raise as many as four (and in rare cases, five) offspring during her life.

Chimpanzees may live for fifty years in the wild.

have scarred ears from fights and scuffles. They can live to be as old as fifty, and they die from some of the same diseases that people get.

Chimpanzees suffer from ulcers, sores, rashes, arthritis, worms, lice, and ticks. They get coughs and colds, especially in the rainy season. Rarely, an epidemic of polio may strike a community, leaving chimpanzees of various ages dead or paralyzed. Thanks to the cooperation among chimpanzees, individuals with a paralyzed arm or leg may still be able to survive for many years.

Chimpanzees have very few predators apart from humans, but a leopard, lion, or baboon sometimes kills an inexperienced or isolated animal. Accidents also account for some deaths. Chimpanzees sometimes fall when stepping onto a dead or broken branch, or while fighting or chasing monkeys in the treetops.

The death of a chimpanzee can have a devastating effect on family members. A chimpanzee under five years of age whose mother dies is unlikely to survive. Older offspring may withdraw for weeks, sitting huddled with their arms clasped around their knees, rocking or plucking at their hair. If a youngster between the ages of five and ten loses its mother, it is likely to take much longer than usual to mature.

Quiet Giants: Gorillas

When a gorilla walks on all fours, its long arms hold its shoulders higher than the rest of its body.

Dian Fossey struggled up the slippery mountainside, cutting away tall clumps of nettles among the tangled forest growth. She was in Rwanda to study gorillas in their misty home, nearly 10,000 feet up the slopes of the Virunga Volcanoes. It was cold, dark, and wet. Her clothes were soaked by sweat and rain, and her boots were caked with mud. Thorns and biting insects added to the misery. Perhaps it isn't surprising that few people had ventured here to observe mountain gorillas, the rarest of the three gorilla subspecies.

Gorillas are the largest living primates. Full-grown male gorillas in zoos can weigh well over 500 pounds and stand about six feet tall. Such captive giants have had too much food and too little exercise, however. The average weight of males in the wild is closer to 380 pounds. Females are much shorter and lighter – about five feet tall and 200 pounds on average. A lot of a gorilla's bulk is muscle, making it incredibly powerful for its size.

Like chimpanzees, gorillas have long arms and short legs. They can walk upright, but their usual way of getting around on the ground is on all fours. The backs of their knuckles, where they rest their weight, have thickened skin. The hands of an adult male are enormous, with fingers the size of bananas. Their big toes are long and help them grip branches when they are climbing.

In addition to being different in size, male and female gorillas are different in color. Males begin to get silvery-gray hair on their backs when they become adults at about ten years of age, whereas females stay blackish-brown. Mature males, often called silver-backs, also grow long, shaggy hair on their arms and lose their chest hair.

Despite their size and fearsome looks, gorillas

A mature male gorilla has a high crest at the top of his skull.

WHERE GORILLAS LIVE

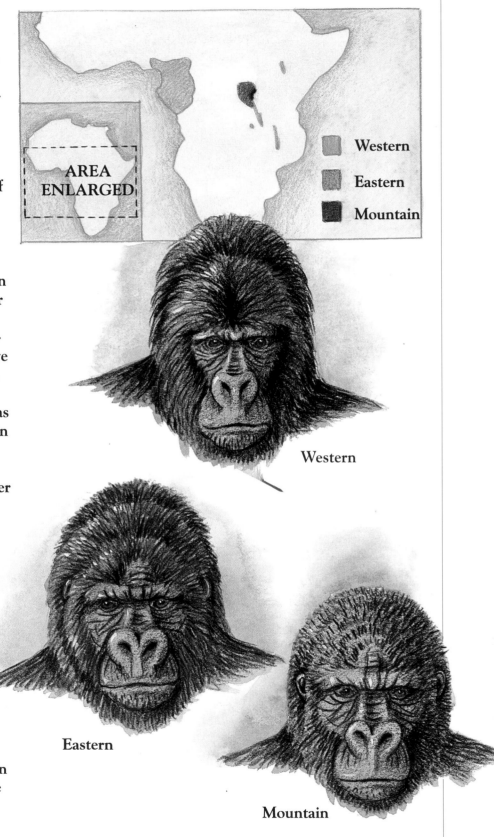

Gorillas live in the dense forests of equatorial Africa, from Nigeria on the west coast to Uganda in the east. There are three different types, or *subspecies*, of gorilla. They look slightly different from one another and live in different parts of Africa.

The commonest and smallest subspecies is the *western lowland gorilla,* which is the type most often seen in zoos. The short hair of this subspecies varies in color from black to grayish-brown, and males often have reddish hair on their heads. There are probably fewer than 40,000 of these gorillas in the wild and about 500 in zoos around the world.

Eastern lowland gorillas are slightly bigger and darker than western lowland gorillas. They also have longer faces with less hair. There are between 3,000 and 5,000 of these gorillas living in the wild.

The rarest subspecies is the *mountain gorilla.* It is larger than the lowland gorilla and has longer, thicker hair, which helps keep it warm in its high, cold forest home. In 1967, there were estimated to be more than 15,000 mountain gorillas, but today there are probably fewer than 700 left.

AREA ENLARGED

Western

Eastern

Mountain

Western

Eastern

Mountain

are quiet, peaceful animals. They are exclusively vegetarian and spend much of the day chewing leaves and stems. They have big molar teeth to grind down tough, fibrous plants, and big stomachs to hold all the bulky vegetation they need to fuel their bodies. An adult gorilla eats from forty to sixty pounds of food per day. The gorilla's "fangs," or canine teeth, may be three inches long in adult males. They use them to tear open tough stems or to frighten enemies. Their strong jaw muscles are attached to a large, bony crest on top of the gorilla's skull. The high crest of a mature male gives his head a dome-shaped appearance.

Gorillas don't have to look very hard to find food – they can hardly move a step in their lush forest home without walking on or brushing past something to eat. Leaves, stems, and shoots make up the majority of their diet, with occasional meals of fruit, bracket fungus, bark, and roots. Among their favorite plants are wild banana, wild celery, stinging nettles, thistles, bamboo, ginger, tapioca, lemonwood, and pepper plants. Dian Fossey and other researchers have tried nibbling many of the gorillas' food plants but found that most of them taste sour or bitter to humans.

Gorillas are vegetarians.

37

Gorillas tend to be leisurely eaters. They often settle down to long meals lasting one to two hours, especially in the mornings, just after they have gotten up. As they sit back and reach for nearby stems or leaves, they munch with a lot of lip smacking, mumbling, and other noises of appreciation. They are neat and careful eaters, taking only the juiciest parts of their food and placing peels, stalks, and other unwanted bits in a neat pile beside them. After a heavy meal on a sunny day, they really do seem to be content, making singing noises that one observer described as a "cross between a dog whining and someone singing in the bath."

Unlike chimpanzees, gorillas have not been seen eating meat in the wild, although they might sometimes eat grubs or insects mixed up with their leaves. Also unlike chimpanzees, they do not use tools to get their food – not because they are less intelligent, but because they don't need them.

Gorillas generally feed and travel on the ground, moving mainly in the afternoon after a morning feed and a midday nap. If it rains heavily during the day, they stop feeding and sit hunched up, waiting with their legs drawn in and their arms folded until the rain stops. They climb trees only to reach particular fruits or leaves, or to get a better view of something, or to sleep for the night.

As sunset approaches, gorillas make nests for sleeping. They lie in their nests on their sides with their knees drawn up, much like humans sleep. Females and young males build their nests less than twenty feet off the ground – much lower than chimpanzees do. Heavy adult males, however, usually sleep on the forest floor or on fallen trees.

Just as the gorillas' pace of life is calmer than that of their active cousins, the chimpanzees, so, too, is their social life less complicated. Gorillas live in small, stable groups, called *troops*. Each troop is based on a family. It usually has only one mature silverback, who acts as the troop's leader. There may be one or two younger males (perhaps the silverback's brothers) and several adult females with youngsters of various ages. In all, there are usually no more than twenty animals in a troop.

Each member of the troop has its place in a hierarchy. The silverback is dominant. If there is more than one silverback, they have an order of rank. Adult males are dominant over females, and females with young are dominant over females without young. The hierarchy helps keep peace and order among the members of a troop. It allows high-ranking animals to gently shift lower-ranking ones from a favorite food site or shelter without the need for fighting.

The members of a troop spend each day together, rarely straying more than a hundred feet apart as they travel, feed, play, or rest. Surrounded by his family, the lead silverback usually sets the day's agenda. Where he goes, the rest follow. As the troop moves unhurriedly through the tangled undergrowth of the forest, they keep in touch by quiet grunts when they can't see one another.

The home range of a gorilla troop is about fifteen to twenty square miles, but the animals typically move less than a mile a day. Through most of the year, they find all the food they need within their range. At certain times, however, they may wander farther than usual to find special delicacies, such as tender young bamboo shoots. Or they may travel out of their range to a salt lick – an area with exposed natural salt deposits, which animals lick to maintain good health.

Relationships between neighboring gorilla troops are usually as easygoing as the relationships within a troop. The ranges of several troops may overlap, and when two troops meet during their wanderings, they

Gorillas live in small family groups.

generally pass each other by without hostility. The only time gorillas fight is when they are defending their troop from danger, or when a rival silverback from another troop attempts to take a female away.

When a troop is threatened, the females and youngsters usually huddle together and rely on the silverback to drive away the intruder. In most cases, the silverback doesn't need to fight. He puts on such a terrifying display that only the bravest opponents stay to watch. The gorilla's former reputation as an aggressive and dangerous animal comes from his chest-thumping show, which is mostly a very successful bluff.

Rarely, two males from different troops may fight, but their fights are not the long and deadly battles of chimpanzees. Gorillas bite, scratch, and slap each other, then retreat. The victor does not chase an opponent who runs away.

Tension comes into the normally placid life of a troop when adolescent animals are ready to start families of their own. Young males wander off to look for mates from other troops, and young females get ready to leave their families. A mature silverback may also raid a neighboring troop to kidnap a new mate.

Like the other great apes, gorillas may breed at any time of year. Most often, females mate with the dominant silverback in their troop. A silverback's daughter may mate with a male who has recently left another troop and is wandering on his own. She may then remain with her troop, or she may go off with her mate to start a troop of their own.

A newborn gorilla weighs between four and five pounds and has pinkish-gray skin with little hair except on the top of its head. It grows quickly on its mother's milk and soon becomes an attractive ball of fur with big, dark eyes and a sweet expression. For the first few months of life, the baby gorilla clings tightly

*A silverback's impressive threat
display warns enemies away.*

A GAME OF BLUFF

Rising on his back legs, a threatened silverback slaps his cupped hands rapidly against his chest, making deep drumming sounds that carry through the forest. This is a warning.

If the intruder stays, the silverback roars while showing his large canine teeth, drops on all fours, and slashes at the vegetation around him with wide sweeps of his arms.

Finally, he rises again, runs quickly sideways toward his opponent, roars, beats his chest, throws around more vegetation, and slaps the ground. His running charge stops just short of the intruder, who, by this time, usually flees in fear. If the intruder remains, however, the silverback may decide it is time for *him* to go, and he will lead his troop away.

with both hands and feet to the hair on its mother's stomach.

Young gorillas develop through the same stages of movement as human babies, but much faster. They can crawl at nine weeks of age, stand by twenty weeks, and walk by thirty-four weeks – an age at which most human babies haven't yet started to crawl. When it is a few months old, a baby gorilla begins to ride around on its mother's back. Younger infants play happily by themselves. They like to experiment with leaves and twigs, often putting them on their heads. Older babies soon find others to play with, as there are often several youngsters of different ages in a troop at any given time.

Gorillas start to learn about food as soon as they are able to walk on their own, although they continue to suckle and depend on their mothers until they are two to three years old. A baby gorilla picks up bits and pieces of food its mother drops and puts them in its mouth. It learns from watching her what is good to eat and where to find it in the forest.

The early years are a risky time of life. Baby gorillas may starve, get diseases, be killed by a predator, or accidentally fall from a tree. Nearly one out of two babies dies before its third birthday.

Between the ages of four and ten, youngsters have a carefree time, playing and learning about the business of being a gorilla. They scamper and frolic together, in lively contrast to the serene and slow-moving adults. Both male and female gorillas are very caring toward the young, and even a big silverback lets them climb on him, pull his hair, and punch his massive bulk with their tiny fists. Only when they near adolescence will he deter them with a stare or a sharp cuff.

A mother gorilla waits four or five years before she becomes pregnant again. By then, her older

A baby gorilla has a most appealing look.

offspring is well on its way to looking after itself. Females show mothering behavior at a young age and often help take care of a younger sibling after it is born. A female gorilla is ready to have her first baby when she is as young as ten. Young males mature a few years later, but they may not be able to mate until they are twenty years of age or older, since they must be big and experienced before they can successfully attract females away from rival silverbacks.

The life of a troop hangs in the balance when the dominant silverback dies. Before that happens, the old male may already have been challenged successfully by a younger silverback. He may then stay on "in retirement" for a year or two, giving up the duties of leader to his successor. A successor may come from the silverback's own troop, or he may be a lone gorilla who has been traveling on his own for several years.

When a new silverback takes over a troop, he may kill any young infants. The mothers who lose their babies will soon become ready to mate again. In this way, the new leader can quickly start his own family and does not have to spend years helping to look after his predecessor's offspring.

Red Apes: Orangutans

Orangutans are the largest tree-living animals in the world.

The hot and humid forests on the islands of Borneo and Sumatra are filled with one of the greatest varieties of plants and animals anywhere on Earth. There, among humming insects, shrill birdsong, brightly colored butterflies, and hundreds of different orchids, the mysterious orangutans sit quietly in the shadows, high among the branches of giant trees.

You might think that a 200-pound ape covered with long, red fur would be an easy thing to observe, but they are surprisingly difficult animals to spot among the green and brown tangle of forest growth. Adding to the problem is the fact that adult orangutans spend much of their time alone, so an observer must look for one animal at a time. Furthermore, orangutans can sit without moving for hours. No wonder that one of the first scientists to study these apes in the forest described them as "shaggy, surly bundles of complete inactivity."

Orangutans, the last of the great apes to be studied in the wild, are the only great apes found in Asia. Compared with chimpanzees and gorillas, orangutans are solitary and slow-moving, and they spend more time in trees. Although usually shy, they don't like being disturbed. When an orangutan spots someone watching it from the forest floor, it often shrieks and shakes the tree. An angry orangutan may tear off branches and throw them down – and one scientist narrowly escaped death when a tree pushed by a large male orangutan crashed only inches from her feet.

A full-grown male orangutan is a memorable sight. About four-and-a-half feet tall and weighing roughly 200 pounds, he is covered with long, thick, reddish-brown hair, which flows over his arms and

The orangutan is the only great ape that lives in Southeast Asia.

shoulders like a shaggy cape. Large fat pads, the size of dinner plates, swell out his cheeks. Hanging under his chin is a large throat pouch. He has a thick body with short legs and very long, powerful arms. When outstretched, his arms can span more than seven feet from fingertip to fingertip. Female orangutans are about half the size of males and do not have cheek pads or throat pouches.

Because of their size, adult males run the risk of tree branches breaking under them. They spend more of their time on the forest floor, where their bulk and strength protect them from predators such as leopards. However, orangutans move awkwardly on the ground. The backs of their hands do not have the thick skin that chimpanzees and gorillas have for walking on their knuckles. And because of their long, curved toes, orangutans tend to walk on the outside edges of their feet, not flat on their soles.

Unlike the other great apes, adult male and female orangutans live separate lives and don't usually

GETTING AROUND THE FOREST

An orangutan's feet have long, fingerlike toes. Shaped like a second pair of hands, they are designed for life in the trees. As the animal swings from branch to branch, its strong fingers and toes curve over the tree limbs like hooks. Its thumbs are short and stubby so they don't get in the way.

An orangutan uses all four limbs equally when climbing. It moves slowly and deliberately, taking care to choose sturdy branches that can support its weight. Like a trapeze artist, it can hang from its feet or its hands, or from one foot and one hand. With its long reach, it can swing across short gaps to get from one tree to another.

stay together except when mating. Females often travel with one or two offspring, but male orangutans move alone through the forest, rarely meeting others. Despite living alone, each male is well aware of his neighbors. He tells others where he is with ear-splitting roars that can carry a mile or more. The chilling sound is amplified by his throat pouch, which swells up like a balloon when he is calling. His calls warn other males to stay away.

Orangutans are more territorial than the other great apes. A male generally keeps to his own small area of forest – about two square miles. (Females have smaller territories and do not call to defend them, as males do.) A male with a territory calls most often when he is near the invisible boundary that separates his part of the forest from that of a neighboring male. Once or twice each day, he shouts his frightening, long-range threats, which may last from one to three minutes. Other males within earshot call back. While two males may both use

A full-grown male orangutan is
a magnificent and powerful
creature.

the same strip of forest along their common border, they take care not to be there at the same time. Their calls help separate them, avoiding meetings that might end in a fight.

When two males do meet, they put on a display to see which of them is more dominant. They roar, stare at each other, and shake branches violently until one of them backs down and retreats. If neither is frightened away by the other, however, they may fight – though such battles are rare. They bite each other's hands and faces and grapple like wrestlers, often falling from the tree during their struggle. They chase each other, glare, grunt, push over tree stumps, and break off branches, continuing until one of them gives up. Fights may last minutes or hours, depending on how evenly matched the apes are. Most adult male orangutans have bite scars on their cheek pads as a result of fights they've been in.

Not all orangutans have territories. Adults of both sexes sometimes wander from one part of the forest to another, passing through different territories as they go. Some of these nomads are traveling to a new food source; others are looking for a mate. Some are searching for an area where they can set up a territory of their own. They may move alone or travel in loose groups, widely spaced apart. Usually the travelers move quietly and quickly when they are near a resident male with a territory.

Being alone for long periods is unusual among primates, but for orangutans, it is their way of life. One researcher followed a female orangutan continuously for a month. In all that time, the ape met only five others, and in most cases she ignored them. She spent a total of only six hours during the month in the company of other orangutans.

Why are orangutans so solitary? The answer probably lies in their feeding habits. Orangutans live mainly on fruits – and being such big animals, they need plenty of them. But fruits in a tropical forest ripen on different trees at different times. To get enough to eat, orangutans may have to travel some distance from one fruiting tree to another. Yet they cannot search a large area each day because they are fairly slow-moving. If they lived in groups, or even in pairs, they would have to share any food they found. By dividing the forest among themselves, each animal has the use of its own small area, which has just enough food for one.

Figs, lychees, acorns, sweet plums, and mangoes are a few of the fruits that orangutans enjoy. Another favorite is durian – a football-size fruit with a thick, thorny rind. Orangutans use their fingers and teeth to rip away the durian's tough skin and get at the juicy pulp inside.

The variety of ripe fruits varies throughout the year, with the peak coming from May to October. Like chimpanzees, orangutans make the most of a crop while it lasts. A big tree may hold thousands of fruits in a good season – so many, in fact, that several orangutans may share it for a few days, in an exception to their general rule. Where there's plenty for all, there's no need to quarrel. In their typical way, though, each animal sits on its own fruit-laden branch and ignores the others.

When fruits are scarce, orangutans eat strips of bark or nibble on buds and flowers. They may chew vine stems to get at the sweet sap inside and then spit out the tough, fibrous remains. Occasionally, an orangutan may raid a bees' nest for its honey. Meat eating is very rare, but researchers once saw a male orangutan take baby squirrels from their nest and eat them.

An orangutan's day begins in the dark, just before dawn, when it gets up from its nest and slips

Orangutans live mainly on fruits – and plenty of them.

away to feed. Females and young orangutans nest overnight as high as seventy feet up in the trees, while mature males usually nest on the ground. They feed most of the morning, often going first to trees in which they had supper the evening before. Around noon, they take a nap, after which they explore the forest for more food. A male may bellow at his neighbors before having another lengthy meal in the late afternoon. Orangutans make new nests every evening and retire around sunset.

As with all great apes, there
is a very strong bond between a
mother orangutan and her baby.

The biggest change in the orangutan's daily routine comes at mating time, when a male and female may spend several days together, courting. Some females are attracted by the calls of a male with a territory, while others appear frightened by these large, noisy males. They respond instead to quieter, younger males without territories. After two animals pair up, they move around and feed together for a few days, often sitting beside each other and nuzzling.

Nearly nine months after mating, the female gives birth to a baby. The bond between the baby and its mother is strong, and this is the only period in its life when an orangutan has close contact with another member of its species. Because adults are solitary, a baby orangutan rarely has other youngsters to play with. For the first year of its life, baby and mother stick close together. During quiet moments when the baby is not asleep, the mother may groom its coat or play with it. When she moves, the infant clings tightly to her fur.

At one year old, the baby orangutan weighs about fifteen pounds. It will depend on its mother's milk for another year, but the mother now begins to press bits of chewed fruit into the baby's mouth when she eats. As the months pass, the baby finds bits of food for itself or shares its mother's meal from time to time. Sometimes, however, the mother seems too occupied with her own business to pay it much attention. Like a human baby, the little orangutan may scream and throw a temper tantrum to get its mother's attention, or to get a piece of her juicy mango.

A two-year-old youngster is able to build a little nest for itself during the day, although it still shares its mother's nest at night. It can now climb and swing with more confidence and plays in nearby branches while its mother takes a nap. The mother encourages the youngster's climbing skills, lifting it up onto branches and holding its hands.

During the third year, ties between mother and offspring begin to loosen. Occasionally, the two of them may meet other orangutans in a fruit tree. Taking advantage of the rare opportunity, youngsters leave their mothers and play together, chasing or grappling with one another and swinging through the branches. As the young ones get carried away with their games and the mothers are intent on eating, each seems to forget about the other. A scientist once saw a mother finish eating and leave a fruit tree by herself. When her youngster realized she was gone, it scrambled frantically after her, screaming loudly.

By the age of four or five, a young orangutan is ready for an independent life. The key break with its mother comes when it builds its own nest for the night. At first, it will make its nest only a few feet from hers. Gradually, it spends the nights farther away.

Four years after her last mating, the mother is ready to mate again. When her next infant arrives, the first-born can no longer expect much attention from its mother. If it hasn't already begun to sleep alone, it must do so now, as the new baby shares the mother's nest. If the older one tries to bunk in with the mother as usual, she will push it away. Although no longer dependent on its mother, a five-year-old orangutan continues to stay in her territory for another year or so. It may spend much of the day on its own, but it usually returns to make its nest within sight of her at night. As the young orangutan gets older, it may follow other adults or keep company with another orangutan of its own age for several days at a time.

At adolescence, about seven years of age, a male orangutan leaves its mother's territory. A young female still follows her mother for another year or so, sometimes playing with a younger brother or sister

and learning the skills of raising a baby. This learning period is very important, because when a female has her own first baby, she will be on her own.

Female orangutans reach their adult weight at about eight years of age but may not mate for another year or two. Males continue to grow for a few more years and are not physically mature and ready to mate until they are twelve to fifteen years old. Their hair grows longer and darker during this period, and they develop cheek pads and a throat pouch. Orangutans in zoos have lived for as long as fifty-seven years, but in the wild they probably do not survive much past forty.

At adolescence, a male orangutan sets off on his own.

Apes in Their Environment

When Jane Goodall first went to Tanzania to study chimpanzees in 1960, she was not a typical scientist. At that time, researchers of animal behavior often assumed that all members of a species act much alike. They referred to individual animals as "it," not as "he" or "she." They certainly didn't give each animal its own name, and they were wary of suggesting that animals might have humanlike moods and motives.

As an inexperienced student, Goodall recorded whatever she saw. It was soon obvious to her that every chimpanzee has its own character, and that the behavior of one or two individuals can influence the behavior of others in their group. Chimpanzees do not act in easily predictable ways. They do not have automatic reactions to particular situations. Their behavior varies from one chimp to another, and from one year to the next. The key to understanding chimpanzees, Goodall concluded, was to accept that they are no more alike than one person is to another.

In many ways, studies of great apes in the wild have led to a breakthrough in the way we think about other animals. Our discoveries about apes have helped narrow the huge gap that people once thought existed between human beings and all other species.

But we have begun to learn the secrets of the great apes just at the time in history when human activities threaten to exterminate chimpanzees, gorillas, and orangutans in the wild. Only fifty years ago, there were *millions* of chimpanzees in Africa. Today, there are fewer than 250,000 left. There are no chimps at all in four of the African countries where they were once very common, and their numbers are dropping rapidly in every other country where they are still found. The same sad story is true for gorillas and orangutans.

Do chimpanzees and other apes have thoughts and feelings, like humans?

THE DISAPPEARING RANGE OF THE ORANGUTAN

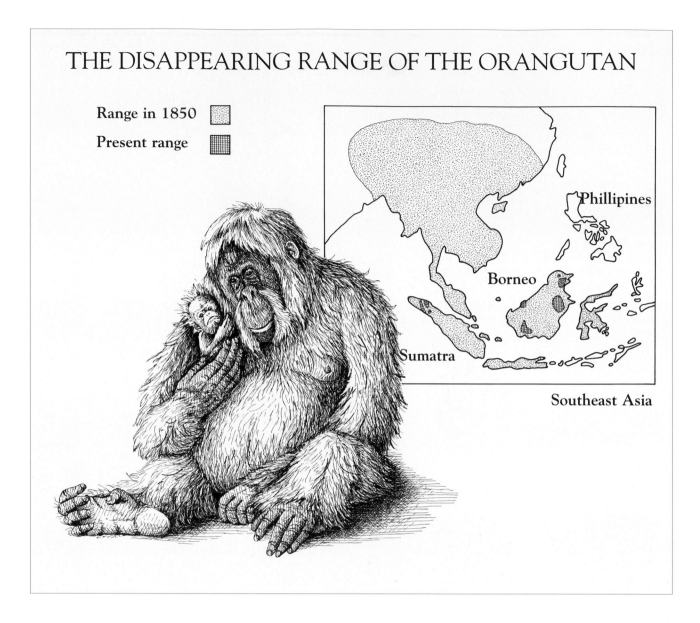

Range in 1850

Present range

Phillipines

Borneo

Sumatra

Southeast Asia

Why are the great apes disappearing? There are several reasons. Although it is illegal in most countries to buy or sell great apes, many are still caught by poachers and sent abroad to be sold as pets, put in zoos or circuses, or used in medical research. For every young ape that reaches its destination alive, as many as ten others die. Some die while being transported, from disease, lack of food, or shock and despair at being captured and separated from their families. Some are killed during the hunt. Other apes are hunted and killed for their meat or for their body parts and skins. People buy parts of apes as trophies and souvenirs, or because they believe certain body parts have magical or medical powers.

Because all the great apes live in forests, the greatest threat to their survival is the chain saw. In many parts of the tropics, forests are being cut down at a rapid rate to provide wood for fuel and building or to clear more land for farmers. Where there were once vast areas of forest, there are now small islands of trees surrounded on all sides by farms. Isolated in their pockets of forest, communities of great apes are cut off from contact with their neighbors. Adding to the threat, apes that leave the forest to feed on crops in the fields are often shot as pests.

In many parts of Africa, the human population is growing quickly. With more human mouths to feed every year, the pressure to cut forests increases.

Deforestation is the greatest threat to the survival of all apes, including these mountain gorillas.

61

Unless we rapidly change our behavior, great apes will soon disappear from the wild places where they have lived for millions of years.

Amid all this destruction, there are attempts to save the great apes. In Borneo, young orangutans whose parents have been killed are being raised in a refuge and helped to return to the forest. In many countries, the money brought by tourism has encouraged governments to protect the wild animals that tourists come to see. Educators are teaching the value of wildlife to children in countries where great apes live. Most of these children have never seen an ape in the wild. In North America and Europe, strict controls on importing apes have reduced the demand for them, and captive apes are being bred in zoos.

The future of the great apes is still uncertain, however. Political unrest in countries where they live makes it difficult to protect them. The spread of guns and the tracks made by log-hauling machines make it easier for poachers to get into the forests and kill them. Even tourism poses a threat, as diseases brought in by visitors could spread to a group of apes and quickly wipe them out.

It has been less than 10 million years since our ancestors separated from those of chimpanzees and gorillas. The great apes are our closest animal relatives, and they still have a lot more to teach us. Should we allow them to disappear from the wild because we continue to destroy their last remaining homes? Or should we extend a helping hand to protect the great apes and their environment so these magnificent creatures may continue to share the planet with us?

INDEX

Numbers in italics refer to illustrations and photographs.